FIRST STEPS IN CODING

WHAT'S BRANCHING?
A BIRTHDAY ADVENTURE!

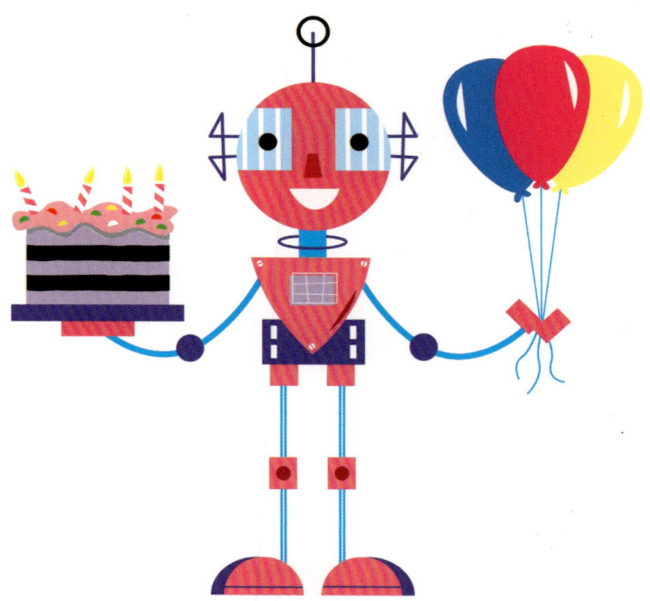

BY KAITLYN SIU AND MARCELO BADARI

WAYLAND
www.waylandbooks.co.uk

First published in Great Britain in 2022
by Wayland
Copyright © Hodder and Stoughton, 2022
All rights reserved.

Editors: Elise Short and Grace Glendinning
Cover design: Peter Scoulding
Inside design: Emma DeBanks

HB ISBN: 978 1 5263 1575 5
PB ISBN: 978 1 5263 1576 2

Printed and bound in China

Wayland, an imprint of
Hachette Children's Group
Part of Hodder and Stoughton
Carmelite House
50 Victoria Embankment
London EC4Y 0DZ

An Hachette UK Company
www.hachette.co.uk
www.hachettechildrens.co.uk

London Borough of Enfield	
91200000758476	
Askews & Holts	23-Feb-2022
J005.13 JUNIOR NON-F	
ENTOWN	

The website addresses (URLs) included in this book were valid at the time of going to press. However, it is possible that contents or addresses may have changed since the publication of this book. No responsibility for any such changes can be accepted by either the author or the Publisher.

WHAT'S BRANCHING?

Let's find out! We'll help super robot Pixel plan a perfect party for Jet, and learn cool coding skills while we do. It's party time, super coders!

Jet can't wait for her birthday to come. On 16 November she will be 800 years old! (That's 8 years old in human years.)

Pixel is Jet's best friend. She is planning an amazing birthday party for Jet.

Pixel wants to pick the perfect spot for Jet's birthday party. There are so many places to choose from!

Should they go to the cinema?

Should they go roller-skating?

Should they go to the dinosaur museum?

Pixel thinks about what Jet would like best.

She knows that Jet loves playing outside and thinks that the best place for the party would be the park.

Pixel starts making plans for activities to do on Jet's big day. She decides to include some of Jet's favourites, such as football, water balloons and dancing.

water balloons

football

dancing

Another robot friend, Bolt, helps Pixel write invitations to the party.

Oh no! Pixel realises that a park party will be ruined by rainy weather. She decides she should have a back-up plan. Pixel needs to use her robot brain to think like a computer.

Computers have back-up plans built into their code so that they can run smoothly, no matter what happens.

Computers make choices based on what *is happening*, or what *has happened*. These are called the **conditions**.

So Pixel creates a back-up plan and writes it down on each invitation.

IF it is raining, THEN the party will move to the community centre next to the park.

In computer language, writing back-up plans in code is called **branching**. In our lives, we use branching all the time to make choices. We branch using **IF/THEN statements**, just like a computer!

If it's raining,

then we bring an umbrella.

If it's sunny,

then we wear sunglasses.

The weather outside and how we feel are examples of conditions. Branching simply means making a choice based on the conditions.

Now that Pixel has settled on two possible spots for the party, she wants to get started on an amazing birthday cake for Jet.

Pixel reads the recipe. Look – she's found a **branch** in the recipe!

The recipe says:

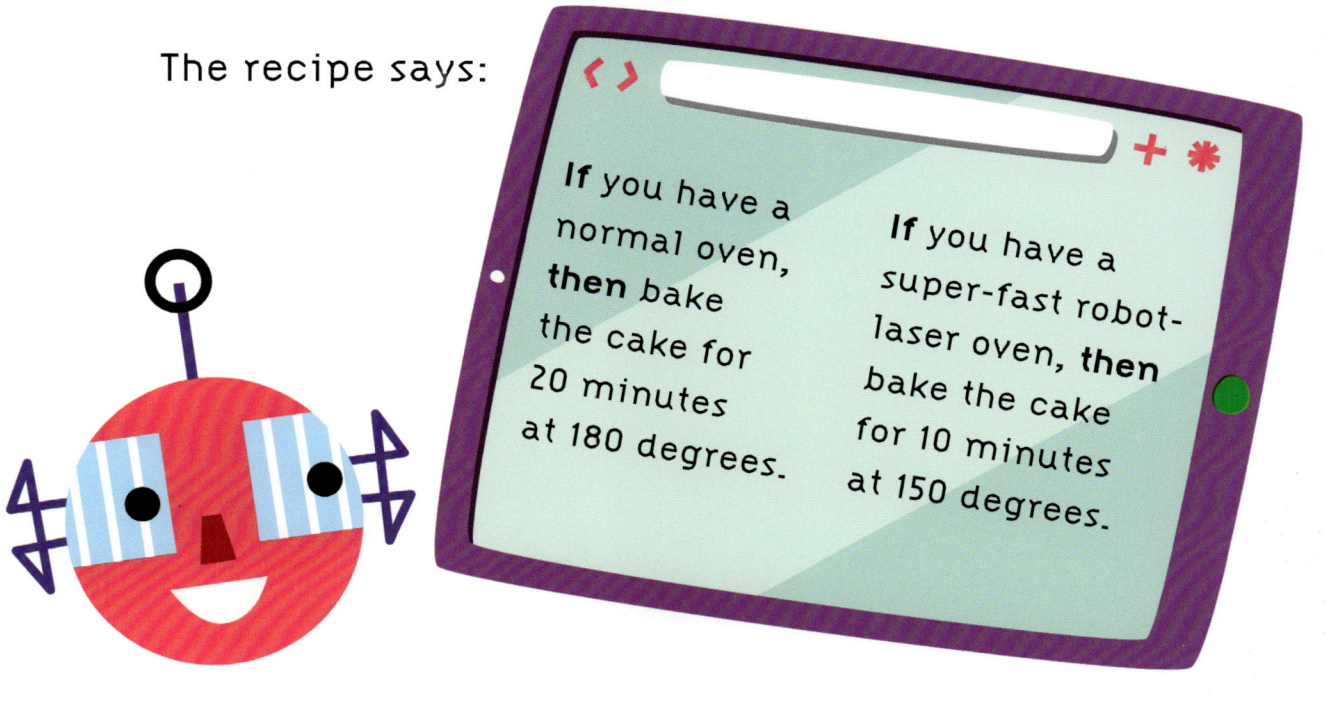

If you have a normal oven, **then** bake the cake for 20 minutes at 180 degrees.

If you have a super-fast robot-laser oven, **then** bake the cake for 10 minutes at 150 degrees.

This recipe gives different **instructions** based on the type of oven you have. That's a branch!

Pixel has a super-fast robot-laser oven, so she sets it to 150 degrees to bake the cake.

Pixel starts blowing up balloons for the party while the cake is in the oven.

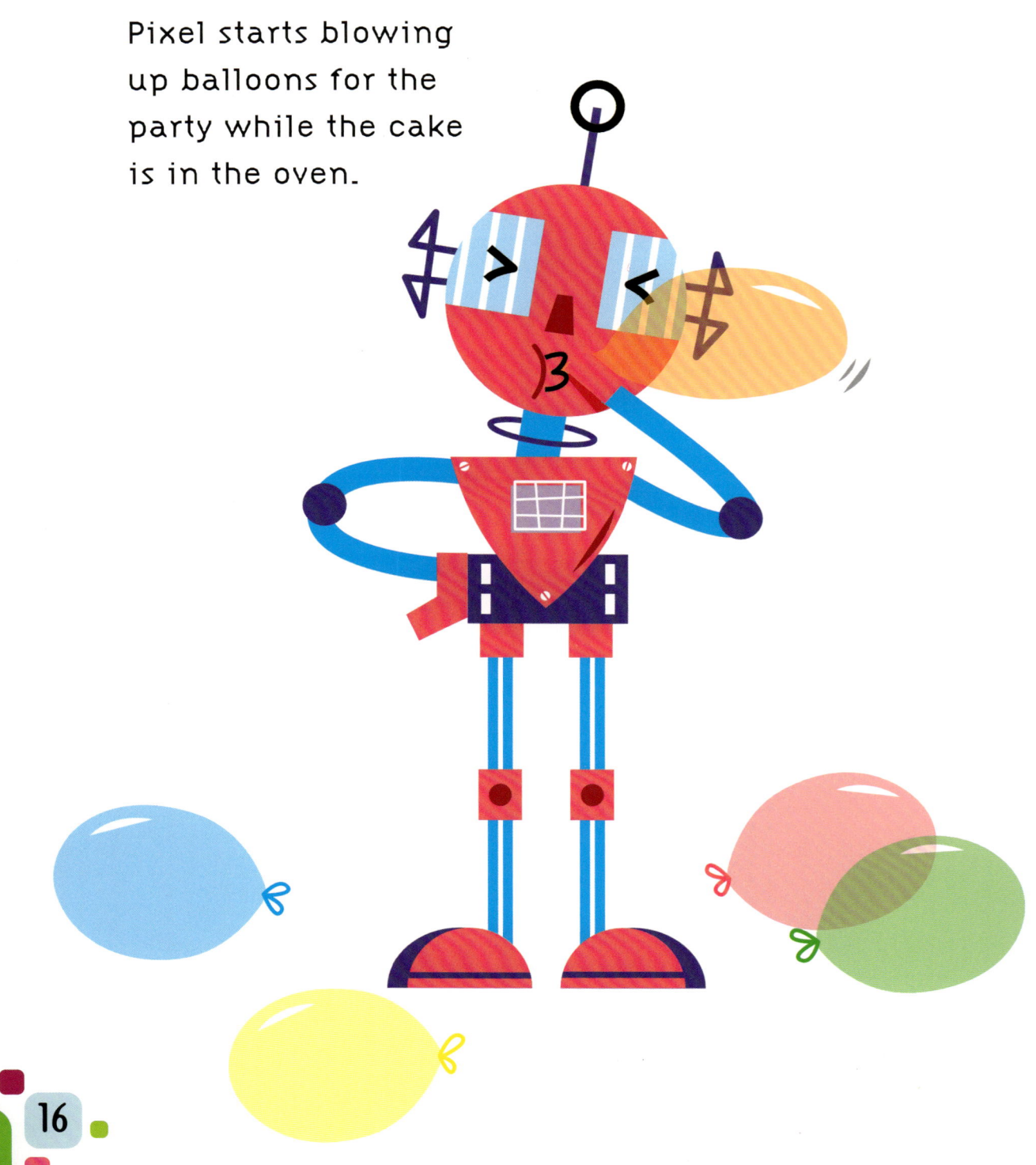

After a while, she smells something burning.

Pixel takes out the burnt cake.

She looks at her timer and sees that instead of setting it for 10 minutes, she accidentally set it for 100 minutes.

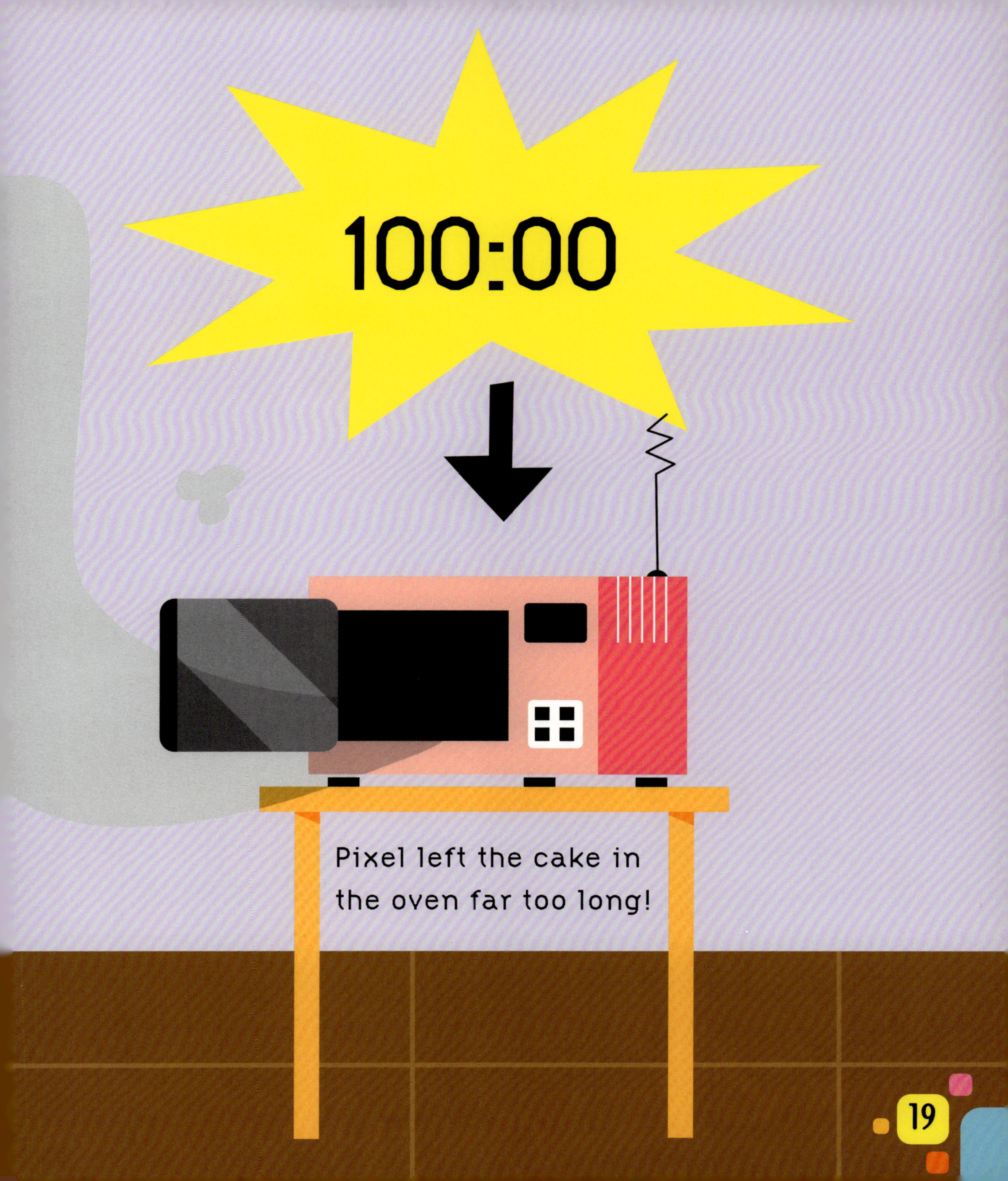

Pixel left the cake in the oven far too long!

In computer coding, mistakes are called **bugs**.

When coders fix problems in their code, it's called **debugging**.

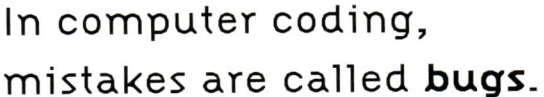

But coders don't need a net to catch these bugs. Coders use their brains!

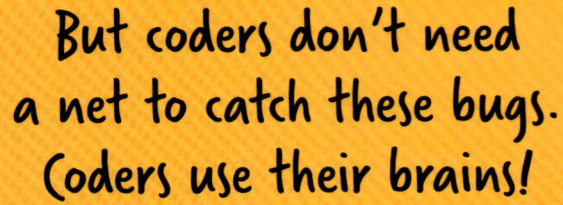

Pixel must debug her cake-making code and try again.

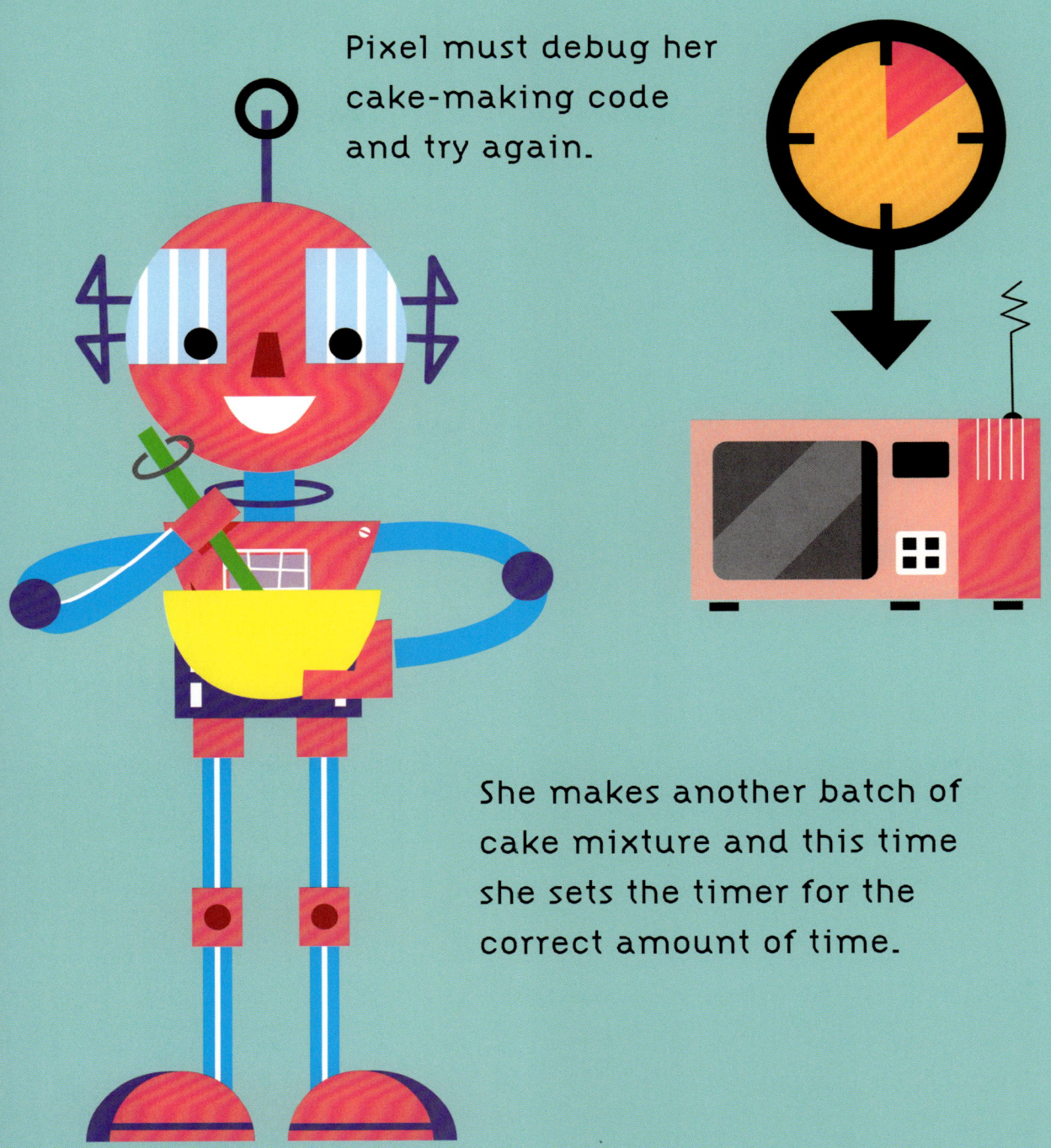

She makes another batch of cake mixture and this time she sets the timer for the correct amount of time.

Brrring!!!

The timer rings. With the debugged code, this branch of the recipe cooked the cake perfectly.

Pixel begins decorating the cake with Jet's favourite colours. She can't wait to show everyone at the party tomorrow!

Finally, it's the day of Jet's birthday party. It's a beautiful sunny day and Pixel is excited to be able to have the party at the park.

Jet and her friends arrive at the park. They all have fun playing party games together.

Branches help computers (and us!) to make the best choices by looking at what is happening.

PARTY TIME

IS THE SUN SHINING?

Branching helps us to be ready for whatever might happen.

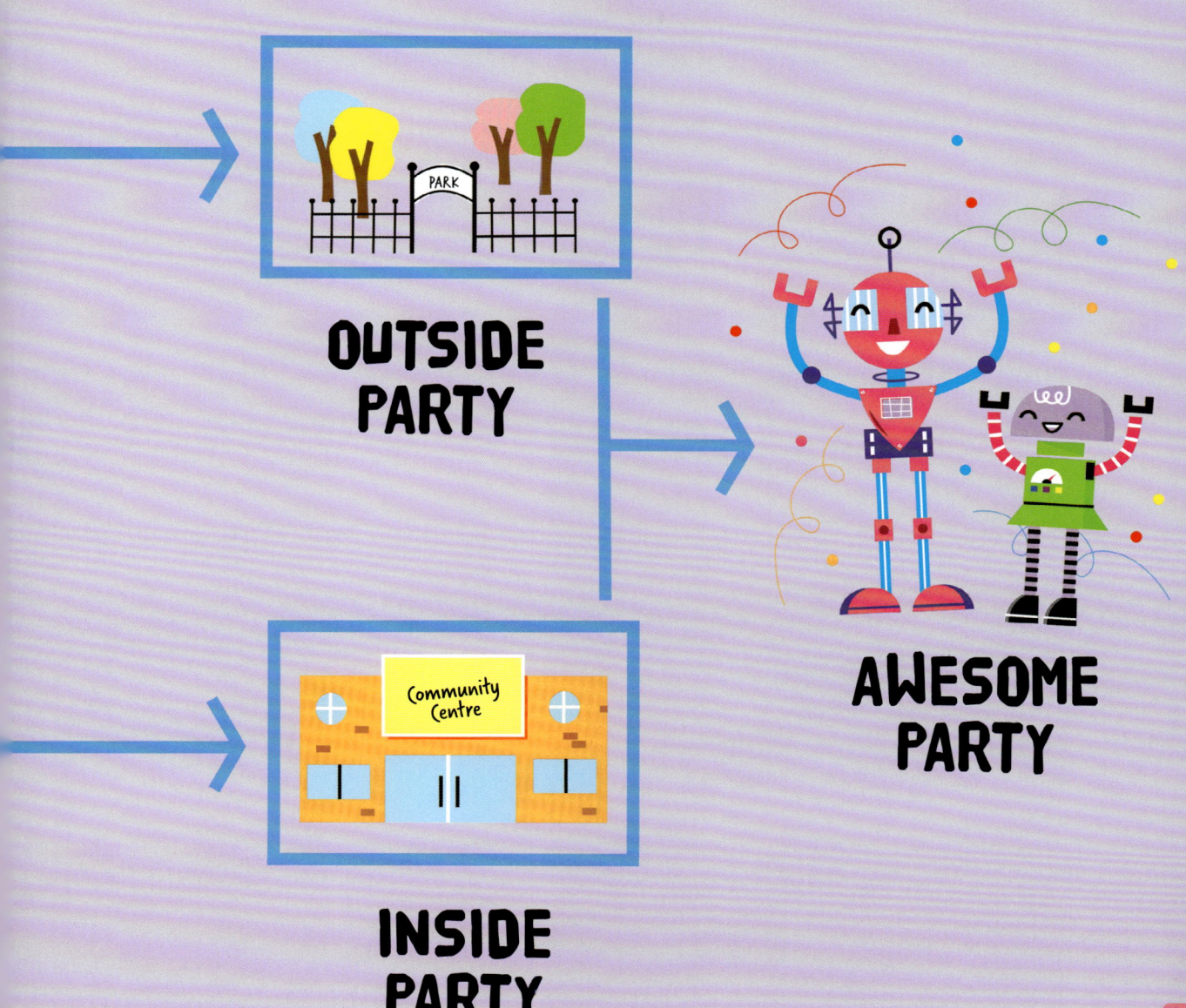

Now it's your turn!

Use your finger to trace a line to the correct branch.

IF

 ... it's cold ...

 ... you are happy ...

 ... you are tired ...

 ... it's hot ...

 ... you are sad ...

 ... you are full of energy ...

 # THEN

... smile!

... wear a T-shirt!

... wear a jacket!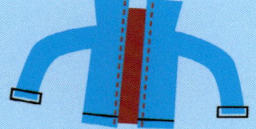

... run around!

... cry!

... sleep!

GLOSSARY

Branch: an instruction that tells a computer to do a certain step, depending on the conditions

Branching: making a decision depending on what is happening or what has happened

Bug: a problem or mistake in coding instructions

Condition: a situation that is happening or has happened, or the current state of something

Debug: find and solve a problem in coding instructions

IF/THEN statements: coding instructions that tell a computer what to do based on the conditions

Instructions: information that tells us what to do

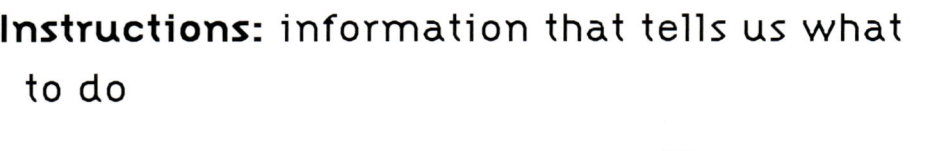

GUIDE FOR TEACHERS, PARENTS AND CARERS

Young children can learn the basic concepts of coding. These concepts are the foundation of computer science, as well as other important skills, such as critical thinking and problem solving.

Branching means making decisions based on the conditions present. Branches are based on 'if/then' conditional statements. Conditionals are the way that computers make decisions.

In this book, students learn all about branching. We use the concept of planning a birthday party, taking into account various conditions, to explain this task.

If you are looking for a supplementary activity, consider this cause-and-effect activity using glow sticks:

www.teachyourkidscode.com/cause-and-effect-activity-dark/

INDEX

B
back-up plan 10–12, 26–27
birthday party 24–27
Bolt 9
branching 3, 12–13, 15,
   21–22, 26–29
bugs 20–21

C
cake 14–23
conditions 10, 13

D
debugging 20–22

I
IF/THEN statements 12, 31
instructions 15

J
Jet 3–9, 14, 23–26

P
party plan 3, 5–11, 14
Pixel 3, 5–11, 14–21,
   23–24